365

Salutes to America

by Kathy Wagoner

SOURCEBOOKS, INC.
NAPERVILLE, ILLINOIS

Published by Sourcebooks, Inc.
P.O. Box 4410, Naperville, Illinois 60567-4410
(630) 961-3900
FAX: (630) 961-2168

ISBN 1-57071-702-8

Printed and bound in the United States of America

DR   10   9   8   7   6   5   4   3   2

Here in the United States we enjoy freedom as a way of life. Our nation is a land of many cultures and diverse voices united by our strong national pride. This gift of democracy is ours to celebrate, to protect, and to pass on. We salute America and the courage, dedication, and heroism of our great country.

We hold these truths to be self-evident, that all men are created equal, that they are endowed by their Creator with certain unalienable Rights, that among these are Life, Liberty and the pursuit of Happiness.

—Declaration of Independence, in Congress, July 4, 1776

If you take advantage of everything America has to offer, there's nothing you can't accomplish.

—Geraldine Ferraro

The fabulous country—
the place where miracles
not only happen, but where
they happen all the time.

—Thomas Wolfe

Territory is but the body of a nation. The people who inhabit its hills and valleys are its soul, its spirit, its life.

-James A. Garfield

The true Republic: men,
their rights, and nothing
more; women, their
rights, and nothing

less.

-Susan B. Anthony

Off with your hat, as the flag goes by! And let the heart have its say; you're man enough for a tear in your eye that you will not wipe away.

—Henry Cuyler Bunner

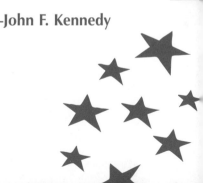

And so, my fellow Americans: ask not what your country can do for you—ask what you can do for your country.

—John F. Kennedy

5

Our institutions of freedom will not survive unless they are constantly replenished by the faith that gave them birth.

—John Foster Dulles

Sometimes people call me an idealist. Well, that is the way I know I am an American. America is the only idealistic nation in the world.

—Woodrow Wilson

In the truest
sense, freedom
cannot be bestowed;
it must be achieved.

-Franklin D. Roosevelt

A little rebellion now and then is a good thing, and as necessary in the political world as storms in the physical.

-Thomas Jefferson

We on this continent should never forget that men first crossed the Atlantic not to find soil for their ploughs but to secure liberty for their souls.

—Robert J. McCracken

America is a tune. It must
be sung together.

—Gerald Stanley Lee

Liberty is the one thing you cannot give love unless you are willing to give it to others.

—William Allen White

This, then, is the state of the union: free and restless, growing and full of hope. So it was in the beginning. So it shall always be, while God is willing, and we are strong enough to keep the faith.

—Lyndon B. Johnson

A real patriot is
the fellow who
gets a parking
ticket and rejoices
that the system works.

-Bill Vaughn

No nation can be
destroyed while it
possesses a good
home life.

-Josiah Gilbert Holland

A free, virtuous, and enlightened people must know full well the great principles and causes upon which their happiness depends.

—James Monroe

Freedom means self-expression and the secret of freedom is courage. No man ever remains free who acquiesces in what he knows to be wrong.

—Harold J. Laski

19

While democracy must have its organization and controls, its vital breath is individual liberty.

—Charles Evans Hughes

Democracy means not, "I am as good as you are," but "You are as good as I am."

—Theodore Parker

I look upon the whole world as my fatherland.
I look upon true patriotism as the brotherhood of man and the service of all to all.

—Helen Keller

Ours is the only country
deliberately founded
on a good idea.

-John Gunther

Everything that is really great and inspiring is created by individuals who labor in freedom.

—Albert Einstein

I wish that every human life might be pure transparent freedom.

—Simone de Beauvoir

Good grants liberty only to those who love it, and are always ready to guard and defend it.

—Daniel Webster

The principal advantage of a democracy is a general elevation in the character of the people.

—James Fenimore Cooper

A patriot is one who wrestles for the soul of her country as she wrestles for her own being.

-Adrienne Rich

We need an America with the wisdom of experience. But we must not let America grow old in spirit.

-Hubert H. Humphrey

A man's feet should be planted in his country, but his eyes should survey the world.

—George Santayana

The Constitution of the United States is the result of the collected wisdom of our country.

—Thomas Jefferson

You have to love a nation that celebrates its independence every July 4, not with a parade of guns, tanks, and soldiers who file by the White House in a show of strength and muscle, but with family picnics where kids throw Frisbees, the potato salad gets iffy, and the flies die from happiness. You may think you have overeaten, but it is patriotism.

—Erma Bombeck

Patriotism is the vital condition
of national permanence.

—George William Curtis

It does not require a lawyer
to interpret the
provisions of the
Bill of Rights. They
are as clear as the
Ten Commandments.

-Herbert Hoover

I like to see a man proud of the place in which he lives. I like to see a man who lives in it so that his place will be proud of him.

-Abraham Lincoln

We want no war of conquest. War should never be entered upon until every agency of peace has failed.

—William McKinley

The only thing we have to fear is fear itself.

—Franklin D. Roosevelt

ternal vigilance is the price of liberty.

—Wendell Phillips

If you expect people to
be ignorant and free
you expect what never
was and never will be.

—Thomas Jefferson

Then join hand in hand, brave Americans all! By uniting we stand, by dividing we fall.

-John Dickinson

All free governments
are managed by the
combined wisdom
and folly of the
people.

-James A. Garfield

Our reliance is in the love of liberty...Our defense is in the spirit which prizes liberty as the heritage of all men, in all lands everywhere.

—Abraham Lincoln

What makes a nation in the beginning is a good piece of geography.

—Robert Frost

Here [in America] individuals of all nations are melted into a new race of men.

—Michel Guillaume Jean de Crevecoeur

One heart, one hope, one destiny,
one flag from sea to sea.

—Kate Brownlee Sherwood

Patriotism, to be truly American, begins with human allegiance.

-Norman Cousins

Eternal vigilance is the condition, not only of liberty, but of everything which as civilized men we hold dear.

-August Heckscher

We admit of no government by divine right; the only legitimate right to govern is an express grant of power from the governed.

—William Henry Harrison

The Bill of Rights, contained in the first ten amendments to the Constitution, is every American's guarantee of freedom.

—Harry S. Truman

The only thing that has ever distinguished America among the nations is that she has shown that all men are entitled to the benefits of law.

—Woodrow Wilson

We here highly resolve that this nation, under God, shall have a new birth of freedom, and that government of the people, by the people, for the people, shall not perish from the earth.

—Abraham Lincoln

Every man who
expresses an
honest thought is
a soldier in the army
of intellectual liberty.

-Robert G. Ingersoll

Courage is the price
that Life extracts for
granting peace.

-Amelia Earhart

We know the best way to enhance freedom in other lands is to demonstrate here that our democratic system is worthy of emulation.

—Jimmy Carter

There is but one element of the government, and that is the people. From this element spring all governments. "For a nation to be free, it is only necessary that she wills it."

—John Adams

Ours is not only a fortunate people but a very common sensical people, with vision high but their feet on the earth, with belief in themselves and faith in God.

—Warren G. Harding

Liberty without learning is always in peril and learning without liberty is always in vain.

—John F. Kennedy

You belong to your country as you belong to your own mother.

-Edward Everett Hale

How important it is for us to recognize and celebrate our heroes and she-roes!

-Maya Angelou

No people can be bound to acknowledge and adore the Invisible Hand which conducts the affairs of men more than those of the United States.

—George Washington

Our country has liberty without license and authority without despotism.

—James Gibbons

Where men cannot freely convey their thoughts to one another, no other liberty is secure.

—William Ernest Hocking

It is the flag just as much of the man who was naturalized yesterday as of the men whose people have been here many generations.

—Henry Cabot Lodge

It is sweet to serve one's country by deeds, and it is not absurd to serve her by words.

-Sallust

There is no freedom on
earth or in any star
for those who
deny freedom
to others.

-Elbert Hubbard

One flag, one land, one heart, one hand, one nation, evermore!

—Oliver Wendell Holmes

Our average fellow-citizen is a sane and healthy man, who believes in decency and has a wholesome mind.

—Theodore Roosevelt

In democracy, the individual enjoys not only the ultimate power but carries the ultimate responsibility.

—Norman Cousins

Peace and friendship with
all mankind is our wisest
policy, and I wish we may
be permitted to pursue it.

—Thomas Jefferson

The unity of
freedom has
never relied on the
uniformity of opinion.

-John F. Kennedy

We are fighting [World War II] because we have the best way of life yet learned by mankind and we want to preserve it.

-Philip Wylie

The commands of democracy are as imperative as its privileges and opportunities are wide and generous. Its compulsion is upon us.

—Woodrow Wilson

Whatever America hopes
to bring to pass in the world
must first come to pass in the
heart of America.

—Dwight D. Eisenhower

I hope to find my country in the right; however, I will stand by her, right or wrong.

—John J. Crittenden

I have been seeing a lot of Americans lately, and they all seem to have that kind of fervour which means aiding and not hindering life.

—Robert Hugh Benson

Our government
wasn't created
to be efficient. It
was created to
preserve the individual.

-Sam Ervin

Let our object be, our country, our whole country, and nothing but our country.

-Daniel Webster

What we need are critical lovers of America—patriots who express their faith in their country by working to improve it.

—Hubert H. Humphrey

The Yankee is one who, if he once gets his teeth set on a thing, all creation can't make him let go.

—Ralph Waldo Emerson

It is the love of country that has lighted and that keeps glowing the holy fire of patriotism.

—J. Horace McFarland

The first requisite of a good
citizen in this republic of ours
is that he shall be able and
willing to pull his weight.

—Theodore Roosevelt

What the people
want is very
simple. They want
an America as good
as its promise.

-Barbara Jordan

We can't all be
Washingtons, but we
can all be
patriots.

-Charles F. Browne

The advice nearest to my heart and deepest in my conviction is, that the Union of the states must be cherished and perpetuated.

—James Madison

Liberty, when it begins to take root, is a plant of rapid growth.

—George Washington

Two cheers for democracy: one because it admits variety and two because it permits criticism.

—E. M. Forster

The ballot is stronger
than the bullet.

—Abraham Lincoln

I venture to suggest that patriotism is not a short and frenzied outburst of emotion but the tranquil and steady dedication of a lifetime.

-Adlai Stevenson

I love America more than
any other country in
this world; and,
exactly for this
reason, I insist on
the right to
criticize her perpetually.

-James Baldwin

I shall know but one country. The ends I aim at shall be my country's, by God's and Truth's. I was born an American; I live an American; I shall die an American.

—Daniel Webster

They did not only leave the old world, they repudiated it. Americans start from scratch.

—Thornton Wilder

The idealists and visionaries, foolish enough to throw caution to the winds and express their ardor and faith in some supreme deed, have advanced mankind and have enriched the world.

—Emma Goldman

He loves his country
best who strives to
make it best.

—Robert G. Ingersoll

Patriotism is just loyalty to friends, people, families.

-Robert Santos

My affections were first for my own country, and then, generally, for all mankind.

-Thomas Jefferson

America is much more than a geographical fact. It is a political and moral fact—the first community in which men set out in principle to institutionalize freedom, responsible government, and human equality.

—Adlai Stevenson

America is great because America is good. And if America ever ceases to be good, America will cease to be great.

—Alexis de Tocqueville

In the United States there is more space where nobody is than where anybody is. That is what makes America what it is.

—Gertrude Stein

So far as it depends on the course of this government, our relations of good will and friendship will be sedulously cultivated with all nations.

—John Tyler

The patriot's
blood is the seed
of Freedom's tree.

–Thomas Campbell

Those who deny freedom
to others deserve it
not for themselves.
And, under a just
God, cannot long
retain it.

-Abraham Lincoln

I for one will never concede that we cannot do as much in defense of our freedoms as any enemy may be doing to destroy them.

—Bernard M. Baruch

The government is the strongest of which every man feels himself a part.

—Thomas Jefferson

The inescapable price of liberty is an ability to preserve it from destruction.

—Douglas MacArthur

Loyalty must arise spontaneously from the hearts of people who love their country and respect their government.

—Justice Hugo L. Black

National honor
is national property
of the highest value.

-James Monroe

If I added to their
pride of America, I
am happy.

-Carl Sandburg

America is another name for opportunity. Our whole history appears like a last effort of divine providence on behalf of the human race.

—Ralph Waldo Emerson

The individual owes the exercise of all his faculties to the service of his country.

—John Quincy Adams

If I have to lay an egg for my country, I'll do it.

—Bob Hope

Patriotism is easy to understand in America. It means looking out for yourself by looking out for your country.

—Calvin Coolidge

America cannot be an ostrich with its head in the sand.

-Woodrow Wilson

Let us remember that
our national unity is
a most priceless
asset.

-Gerald Ford

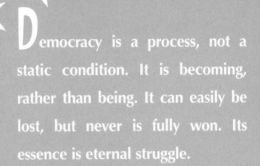

Democracy is a process, not a static condition. It is becoming, rather than being. It can easily be lost, but never is fully won. Its essence is eternal struggle.

—William H. Hastie

It certainly must have been a relief for the women of the country to realize that one could be a woman and a lady and yet be thoroughly political.

—Pearl S. Buck

Liberty, according to my metaphysics...
is a self-determining power in an intellectual
agent. It implies thought and choice and
power.

—John Adams

There are no points of
the compass on the chart
of true patriotism.

—Robert C. Winthrop

There are
inalienable
obligations as well as
inalienable rights.

-Abraham Joshua Herschel

One has the right to be wrong in a democracy.

-Claude Pepper

Our whole duty, for the present,
at any rate, is summed up in the
motto: America First.

—Woodrow Wilson

May the sun in his course visit no land more free, more happy, more lovely, than this our own country!

—Daniel Webster

If a man is fortunate he will, before he dies, gather up as much as he can of his civilized heritage and transmit it to his children.

—Will Durant

'T is not in numbers
but in unity that our
great strength lies.

—Thomas Paine

There is nothing wrong with
America that
the faith, love of
freedom, intelligence,
and energy of her
citizens cannot cure.

-Dwight D. Eisenhower

Democracy cannot be static. Whatever is static is dead.

125

-Eleanor Roosevelt

I shall on all subjects have policy to recommend, but none to enforce against the will of the people.

—Ulysses S. Grant

Ｗe would rather die on our feet than live on our knees.

—Franklin D. Roosevelt

Observe good faith and justice toward all nations. Cultivate peace and harmony with all.

—George Washington

The United States
has to move very fast
even to stand still.

—John F. Kennedy

There is nothing
wrong with
America that
together we can't fix.

-Ronald Reagan

It is not the fact of liberty
but the way in which
liberty is exercised
that ultimately
determines
whether liberty
itself survives.

-Dorothy Thompson

America lives in the heart of every man everywhere who wishes to find a region where he will be free to work out his destiny as he chooses.

—Woodrow Wilson

If we falter in our leadership we may endanger the peace of the world, and we shall surely endanger the welfare of the nation.

—Harry S. Truman

133

You cannot conquer America.

—William Pitt

The great and admirable strength of America consists in this, that America is truly the American People.

—Jacques Maritain

Too much time cannot be spent in a task that is to endure for centuries.

–Augustus Saint-Gaudens

Where liberty dwells,

there is my

country.

-Benjamin Franklin

Science and time and necessity have propelled us, the United States, to be the general store for the world, dealers in everything. Most of all, merchants for a better way of life.

—Lady Bird Johnson

No man is good enough to govern another man without that other's consent.

—Abraham Lincoln

Passivity and not aggressiveness is the dominant trait of the American character.

—Mary McCarthy

It is refreshing to turn to the early incidents of our history, and learn wisdom from the acts of the great men who have gone to their account.

—John McLean

The cement of
this Union is the
heart-blood of
every American.

-Thomas Jefferson

In the field of world
policy I would dedicate
this nation to the
policy of a good
neighbor.

-Franklin D. Roosevelt

America is the only country ever founded on the printed word.

—Marshall McLuhan

The great social adventure of America is no longer the conquest of the wilderness but the absorption of fifty different peoples.

—Walter Lippman

If only we are faithful to our past, we shall not have to fear our future. The cause of peace, justice, and liberty need not fail and must not fail.

—John Foster Dulles

True patriotism hates injustice in its own land more than anywhere else.

—Clarence Darrow

And they who for their country
die shall fill an
honored grave,
for glory lights the
soldier's tomb, and
beauty weeps the brave.

-Joseph Drake

We shall be judged
more by what we do
at home than what
we preach
abroad.

-John F. Kennedy

America is the great melting pot.

—Israel Zanquill

It is, I believe, the destiny of America to produce the first of a new species of man.

—Wyndham Lewis

There is no power on earth equal to the power of free men and women united in the bonds of human brotherhood.

—Walter P. Reuther

A government for the people must depend for its success on the intelligence, the morality, the justice, and the interest of the people themselves.

—Grover Cleveland

I believe in America because we have great dreams–and because we have the opportunity to make those dreams come true.

–Wendell L. Wilkie

Liberty is the breath

of life to nations.

155

-George

Bernard Shaw

Let us have faith in the eternal principles of Americanism; and our example, not less than our sword, will make this world a decent place in which to live.

—Laurette Taylor

The whole inspiration of our life as a nation flows out from the waving folds of this banner.

—Anonymous

He is a poor patriot whose patriotism does not enable him to understand how all men everywhere feel about their altars and their hearthstones, their flags and their fatherland.

—Harry Emerson Fosdick

The winds that blow through the wide sky in these mountains, the winds that sweep from Canada to Mexico, from the Pacific to the Atlantic—have always blown on free men.

—Franklin D. Roosevelt

Liberty is worth
whatever the best
civilization is worth.

-Henry Giles

As President, I have no eyes but constitutional eyes; I cannot see you.

-Abraham Lincoln

Patriotism belongs to the men and women who are the conscience of a nation.

—Guy D. Goff

True patriotism is of no party.

—Tobias Smollett

Peace, commerce, and honest friendship with all nations—entangling alliances with none.

—Thomas Jefferson

Americans believe...in the dignity and strength of common human nature and therefore in democracy and its ultimate triumph.

—Charles W. Eliot

Liberty is always
dangerous, but
it is the safest
thing we have.

-Harry Emerson I

The possession of peace
like ours is not a thing
to be hugged in
selfish enjoyment;
it is endangered
unless it can be
shared.

-W. J. Cameron

Next in importance to freedom and justice is popular education, without which neither freedom nor justice can be permanently maintained.

—James A. Garfield

God bless the USA, so large,
so friendly, and so rich.

—W. H. Auden

For what avail the plough or sail, or land or life, if freedom fail?

—Ralph Waldo Emerson

The greatest glory of a free-born people is to transmit that freedom to their children.

—William Harvard

Flag Day...is a day when we are to recall the things which we should do every day of our lives. There are no days of special patriotism.

-Woodrow Wilson

The free state offers
what a police state
denies—the privacy of
the home, the
dignity and peace
of mind of the
individual.

-William O. Douglas

After order and liberty, economy is one of the highest essentials of a free government...Economy is always a guarantee of peace.

—Calvin Coolidge

There are those, I know, who will say that the liberation of humanity, the freedom of man and mind, is nothing but a dream. They are right. It is the American dream.

—Archibald MacLeish

The United States is like a gigantic boiler. Once the fire is lighted under it there is no limit to the power it can generate.

—Lord Grey

Patriots, in peace, assert the people's right, with noble stubbornness resisting might.

—John Dryden

We hold these truths to be self-evident that all men and women are created equal.

-Elizabeth Cady Stanton

An American is one
who will fight for his
freedom and that

of his neighbor.

-Harold Ickes

$\mathcal{S}$elf-help and self-control are the essence of the American tradition.

—Franklin D. Roosevelt

We must be free not because we claim freedom, but because we practice it.

—William Faulkner

Liberty is not a matter of words, but a positive and important condition of society.

—James Fenimore Cooper

When a great ship cuts through the sea, the waters are always stirred and troubled. And our ship is moving—moving through troubled waters, toward new and better shores.

—Lyndon B. Johnson

Our country, right or wrong. When right, to be kept right; when wrong, to be put right.

-Carl Schurz

If our country is worth
dying for in time of
war, let us resolve
that it is truly
worth living for
in time of peace.

-Hamilton Fish

I was born an American: I will live an American; I shall die an American.

—Daniel Webster

O freedom! First delight of human kind!

—John Dryden

187

A man's country is not a certain area of land, but it is a principle; and patriotism is loyalty to that principle.

—George William Curtis

The cause we supported
was just, and was glorious;
when men fight for freedom,
they must be victorious.

—Joseph Hopkinson

The Declaration of
Independence...
was a vital piece
of practical business,
not a piece of rhetoric.

-Woodrow Wilson

The United States is the only country with a known birthday.

-James G. Blaine

I sometimes think that the saving grace of America lies in the fact that the overwhelming majority of Americans are possessed of two great qualities—a sense of humor and a sense of proportion.

—Franklin D. Roosevelt

We take the stars from heaven, the red from our mother country, separating it by white stripes, thus showing that we have separated from her, and the white stripes shall go down to posterity, representing our liberty.

—George Washington

Too many people expect wonders from a democracy, when the most wonderful thing of all is just having it.

—Walter Winchell

194

Our Constitution professedly rests upon the good sense and attachment of the people. This basis, weak as it may appear, has not yet been found to fail.

—John Quincy Adams

America is a
willingness of the
heart.

-F. Scott Fitzgerald

Liberty has still

a continent to

live in.

-Horace Walpole

Give me your tired, your poor,
your huddled masses yearning to breathe free,
the wretched refuse of your teeming shore,
Send these, the homeless, tempest-tossed to me:
I lift my lamp beside the golden door.

—Emma Lazarus

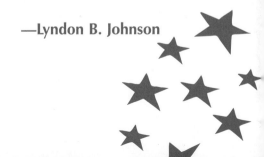

We aspire to nothing that belongs to others. We seek no dominion over our fellow man, but man's dominion over tyranny and misery.

—Lyndon B. Johnson

The country is always stronger than we know in our most worried moments.

—E. B. White

The United States Constitution has proved itself the most marvelous compilation of rules of government ever written.

—Franklin D. Roosevelt

Let us have faith that right
makes might,
and in that faith
let us dare to do
our duty as we
understand it.

-Abraham Lincoln

The greatest happiness of the greatest number is the foundation of morals and legislation.

-Jeremy Bentham

O America because you build for mankind I build for you.

—Walt Whitman

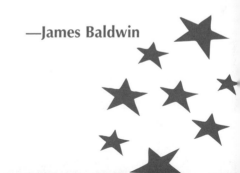

The making of an American begins at the point where he himself rejects all other ties, any other history, and himself adopts the vesture of his adopted land.

—James Baldwin

Americanism consists in utterly believing in the principles of America.

—Woodrow Wilson

I realize that patriotism is not enough. I must have no hatred or bitterness towards anyone.

—Edith Cavell

To embody
human liberty in
workable government,
America was born.

-Herbert Hoover

The spirit of truth and
the spirit of
freedom-they
are the pillars
of society.

-Henrik Ibsen

In short, we must be constantly prepared for the worst and constantly acting for the best—strong enough to win a war and wise enough to prevent one.

—Lyndon B. Johnson

Standing for right when it is unpopular is a true test of moral character.

—Margaret Chase Smith

Then conquer we must, for our cause is just, and this be our motto: "In God is our Trust!"

—Francis Scott Key

Patriotism depends as much on mutual suffering as on mutual success, and it is by that experience of all fortunes and all feelings that a great national character is created.

The care of human life and happiness, and not their destruction, is the first and only legitimate object of good government.

-Thomas Jefferson

Who loves his country

cannot hate

mankind.

-Charles Churchill

America was established not to create wealth but to realize a vision, to realize an ideal—to discover and maintain liberty among men.

—Woodrow Wilson.

Let the people think they govern
and they will be governed.

—William Penn

Let us then stand by the Constitution as it is, and by our country as it is, united, and entire; let it be a truth engraven on our hearts.

—Daniel Webster

The truth is, all might be free if they valued freedom, and defended it as they ought.

—Samuel Adams

Of the many things we have done to democracy in the past, the worst has been the indignity of taking it for granted.

-Max Lerner

The real value of freedom

is not to the minority

that wants to talk, but

to the majority,

that does not

want to listen.

-Zechariah Chafee Jr.

Change is inevitable. In a progressive country change is constant.

—Benjamin Disraeli

No matter that patriotism is too often the refuge of scoundrels. Dissent, rebellion, and all-around hell-rousing remain the true duty of patriots.

—Barbara Ehrenreich

223

I believe in democracy because it releases the energy of every human being.

—Woodrow Wilson

Double—no triple—our troubles and we'd still be better off than any other people on earth.

—Ronald Reagan

Freedom is
nothing else but a
chance to be better.

-Albert Camus

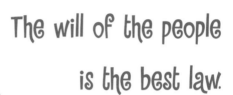

The will of the people

is the best law.

-Ulysses S. Grant

227

Freedom of thought and freedom of speech in our great institutions of learning are absolutely necessary for the preservation of our country.

—John Peter Altgeld

Ours is a land filled with millions of happy homes, blessed with comfort and opportunity. I have no fear for the future of our country. It is bright with hope.

—Herbert Hoover

Y ou gain strength, courage, and confidence by every great experience in which you really stop to look fear in the face. You are able to say to yourself, "I lived through this horror. I can take the next thing that comes along."…You must do the thing you think you cannot do.

—Eleanor Roosevelt

The liberty of a democracy is not safe
if its business system does not provide
employment and produce and distribute
goods in such a way as to sustain an
acceptable standard of living.

—Franklin D. Roosevelt

Wherever public
spirit prevails,
liberty is secure.

-Noah Webster

Not merely a nation
but a nation of
nations.

-Lyndon B. Johnson

The best country for the common man—white or black...if he can't make it here he won't make it anywhere else.

—Eric Hoffer

When good people in any country cease their vigilance and struggle, then evil men prevail.

—Pearl S. Buck

When I signed the Declaration of Independence I had in view not only our independence from England but the toleration of all sects.

—Charles Carroll

Cautious, careful people, always casting about to preserve their reputation and social standing, never can bring about a reform. Those who are really in earnest must be willing to be anything or nothing in the world's estimation.

—Susan B. Anthony

I should like to be able to love my country and to love justice.

-Albert Camus

America, we must remember, is no more than the sum of ourselves.

-John D. Rockefeller III

The spirit of liberty is the spirit which seeks to understand the minds of other men and women; the spirit of liberty is the spirit which weighs their interests alongside its own without bias.

—Learned Hand

The United States is the only great and populous nation-state and world power whose people are not cemented by ties of blood, race, or original language.

—Dorothy Thompson

The primal principle of democracy is the worth and dignity of the individual.

—Edward Bellamy

The best government rests on the people and not on the few, on persons and not on property, on the free development of public opinion and not on authority.

—George Bancroft

I believe in liberty, always and everywhere.

-Robert G. Ingersoll

It is the spirit and not
the form of law that
keeps justice alive. 245

-Earl Warren

Let it be borne on the flag under which we rally in every exigency, that we have one country, one constitution, one destiny.

—Daniel Webster

What's right about America is that although we have a mess of problems, we have a great capacity—intellect and resources—to do something about them.

—Henry Ford II

The history of liberty is the history of resistance...a history of the limitation of governmental power.

—Woodrow Wilson

The land of the free, and
the home of the brave.

—Francis Scott Key

It is an uncompromising devotion to the idea of equal liberty as both the means and end of life that characterizes the liberal spirit.

-H. M. Kallen

This country will not be a
good place for any of
us to live in unless we
make it a good
place for all of
us to live in.

-Theodore Roosevelt

Intellectually I know that America is no better than any other country; emotionally I know she is better than every other country.

—Sinclair Lewis

Patriotism consists not in waving the flag, but in striving that our country shall be righteous as well as strong.

—James Bryce

America is never wholly herself unless she is engaged in high moral principle. We as a people have such a purpose today.

—George Bush

Liberty means responsibility.
That is why most men dread it.

—George Bernard Shaw

Let us never
negotiate out of
fear, but let us
never fear to
negotiate.

-John F. Kennedy

Since when do you have
to agree with people
to defend them
from injustice?

257

-Lillian Hellman

In the new code of laws which I suppose it will be necessary for you to make, I desire you would remember the ladies…If particular care and attention is not paid to the ladies we are determined to foment a rebellion, and will not hold ourselves bound by any laws in which we have no voice, or representation.

—Abigail Adams

At once three outstanding characteristics of the American mind are apparent—equalitarianism, love of freedom, and bounding energy. But the most deep-seated, I am sure, is energy.

—Stephen James Lake Taylor

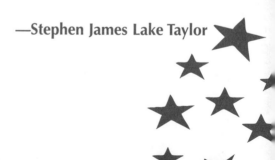

Freedom is still expensive. It still costs money. It still costs blood. It still calls for courage and endurance, not only in soldiers, but in every man and woman who is free and who is determined to remain free.

—Harry S. Truman

Freedom is never voluntarily given by the oppressor; it must be demanded by the oppressed.

—Martin Luther King Jr.

America means
opportunity,
freedom, power.

-Ralph Waldo Emerson

As I would not be a
slave, so I would not
be a master. This
expresses my
idea of democracy.

-Anonymous

You cannot spill a drop of American blood without spilling the blood of the whole world...We are not a nation, so much as a world.

—Herman Melville

A man who is good enough to shed his blood for his country is good enough to be given a square deal afterwards.

—Theodore Roosevelt

265

Liberty exists in proportion to the wholesome restraint; the more restraint on others to keep off from us, the more liberty we have.

—Daniel Webster

The free man, casting
with unpurchased hand
the vote that shakes the
turrets of the land.

—Oliver Wendell Holmes

None who have always been free can understand the terrible fascinating power of the hope of freedom to those who are not free.

-Pearl S. Buck

We have voted as many, but tonight we must face the world as one.

269

-Lyndon B. Johnson

The youth of America is their oldest tradition. It has been going on now for three hundred years.

—Oscar Wilde

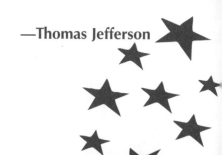

My God! How little do my countrymen know what precious blessings they are in possession of, and which no other people on earth enjoy!

—Thomas Jefferson

Man's capacity for justice makes democracy possible, but man's inclination to injustice makes democracy necessary.

—Reinhold Niebuhr

There is nothing so likely to produce peace as to be well prepared to meet an enemy.

—George Washington

The free way
of life proposes
ends, but it does not
prescribe means.

-Robert Kennedy

The sound of tireless
voices is the price we
pay for the right to
hear the music of
our own opinions.

-Adlai Stevenson

Liberty: One of Imagination's most precious possessions.

—Ambrose Bierce

The most beautiful thing in the world is freedom of speech.

—Diogenes

Patriotism has its roots deep in the instincts and the affections. Love of country is the expansion of filial love.

—David D. Field

Those who won our independence believed liberty to be the secret of happiness and courage to be the secret of liberty.

—Louis D. Brandeis

The history of
every country
begins in the heart
of a man or woman.

-Willa Cather

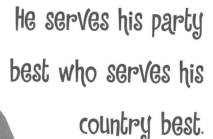

He serves his party
best who serves his
country best.

-Rutherford B. Hayes

281

We must be ready to dare all for our country. For history does not long entrust the care of freedom to the weak or the timid.

—Dwight D. Eisenhower

If we do not make common cause to save the good old ship of the Union on this voyage, nobody will have a chance to pilot her on another voyage.

—Abraham Lincoln

Injustice is relatively easy to bear; what stings is justice.

—H. L. Mencken

285

We have enjoyed so much freedom for so long that we are perhaps in danger of forgetting how much blood it cost to establish the Bill of Rights.

—Felix Frankfurter

The greatest honor which this nation can bestow upon the "unknown hero" would be to live for the things for which he died.

-Anonymous

Those who expect to
reap the blessings
of freedom
must...undergo the
fatigues of
supporting it.

-Thomas Paine

287

Those who are desirous of enjoying all the advantages of liberty themselves, should be willing to extend personal liberties to others.

—Rhode Island Assembly, 1774

The patriots are those who love America enough to wish to see her as a model to mankind.

—Adlai Stevenson

The American Republic was established by the united valor and wisdom of the lovers of liberty from all lands.

—Daniel W. Voorhees

The things required for prosperous labor, prosperous manufactures, and prosperous commerce are three. First, liberty; second, liberty; third, liberty.

—Henry Ward Beecher

We Americans know that freedom, like peace, is indivisible.

-Harold Ickes

A day, an hour of
virtuous liberty, is
worth a whole
eternity of
bondage.

-Joseph Addison

Patriotism is your conviction that this country is superior to all other countries because you were born in it.

—George Bernard Shaw

I only regret that I have but one life to lose for my country.

—Nathan Hale

Justice is the bread of the nation,
it is always hungry for it.

—Francois de Chateaubriand

Government laws are needed to give us civil rights, and God is needed to make us civil.

—Rev. Ralph W. Sockman

I know only two tunes; one of them is "Yankee Doodle," and the other isn't.

-Ulysses S. Grant

Only our individual

faith in freedom can

keep us free. **299**

-Dwight D. Eisenhower

Our country is the world—our countrymen are all mankind.

—William Lloyd Garrison

It is the duty of government to make it difficult for people to do wrong, easy to do right.

—William E. Gladstone

There can be no fifty-fifty Americanism in this country. There is room here for only 100 percent Americanism, only for those who are Americans and nothing else.

—Theodore Roosevelt

They [the Americans] are the
hope of this world. They may
become its model.

—Anne Robert Jacques Turgot

The welfare of
America is
closely bound up
with the welfare of
mankind.

-Marquis de Lafayette

All men are born free
and equal, and have
certain natural,
essential, and
unalienable
rights.

305

-Constitution of Massachusetts

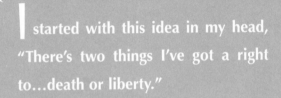

I started with this idea in my head, "There's two things I've got a right to...death or liberty."

—Harriet Tubman

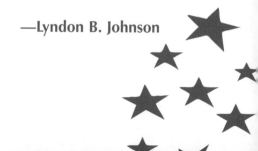

For this is what America is all about. It is the uncrossed desert and the unclimbed ridge. It is the star that is not reached and the harvest that's sleeping in the ground.

—Lyndon B. Johnson

The most important office...that of private citizen.

—Louis D. Brandeis

The blessings of liberty which our Constitution secures may be enjoyed alike by minorities and majorities.

—James K. Polk

All we have of
freedom, all we
use or know-this
our fathers bought us
long and long ago.

-Rudyard Kipling

Not active trade
and victorious armies,
but religion and
morality are the
safeguards of freedom.

-Robert Payne Smith

Nothing is impracticable to this nation, which it shall set itself to do…We are on the brink of more wonders.

—Ralph Waldo Emerson

For every man who lives without freedom, the rest of us must face the guilt.

—Lillian Hellman

We seek peace, knowing that peace is the climate of freedom.

—Dwight D. Eisenhower

Don't spread patriotism too thin.

—Theodore Roosevelt

Freedom exists only where the people take care of the government.

-Woodrow Wilson

I think patriotism is

like charity–it

begins at home.

-Henry James

317

If you want to be free, there is but one way; it is to guarantee an equally full measure of liberty to all your neighbors. There is no other.

—Carl Schurz

Democracy is a very simple principle, and those who speculate about its meaning are those who are not quite willing to accept it. The dictionary defines it as "the rule of the people." Not much more need be said about it.

—Bernard Smith

The cost of freedom is always high, but Americans have always paid it. And one path we shall never choose, and that is the path of surrender, or submission.

—John F. Kennedy

We must be willing, individually and as a nation, to accept whatever sacrifices may be required of us. A people that values its privileges above its principles soon loses both.

—Dwight D. Eisenhower

Americanism means the virtues of courage,

honor, justice,

truth, sincerity, and

hardihood—the virtues

that made America.

-Theodore Roosevelt

The apathy of the born
free man is worse
than the docility of
the born slave.

-Grant Singleton

For mere vengeance I would do nothing. This nation is too great to look for revenge. But for the security of the future I would do everything.

—James A. Garfield

Patriotism knows neither latitude nor longitude. It is not climatic.

—E. A. Storrs

Patriotism is not the mere holding of a great flag unfurled, but making it the goodliest in the world.

—W. J. Linton

327

In the discharge of duties my
guide will be the Constitution,
which I this day swear to
preserve, protect, and defend.

—Zachary Taylor

Guard against
the postures of
pretended patriotism.

-George Washington

Revolution is but
thought carried
into action.

–Emma Goldman

Around our gift of freedom draw the safeguards of thy righteous law.

—John Greenleaf Whittier

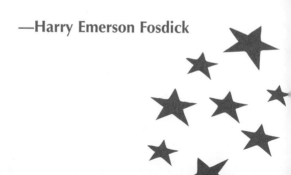

Democracy is based upon the conviction that there are extraordinary possibilities in everyday people.

—Harry Emerson Fosdick

Patriotism means equipped forces and a prepared citizenry.

—Dwight D. Eisenhower

Do not...regard the critics as questionable patriots. What were Washington and Jefferson and Adams but profound critics of the colonial status quo?

—Adlai Stevenson

justice delayed

is democracy denied.

-Robert Kennedy

I am not a Virginian,

but an American.

335

-Patrick Henry

A country fit for liberty—for men who love their fellow men.

—Woodbury Pulsifer

I hope ever to see America among the foremost nations in examples of justice and liberality.

—George Washington

Human freedom is not a gift of man. It is an achievement by man; and, as it was gained by vigilance and struggle, so it may be lost in indifference and supiness.

—Harry F. Byrd

Liberty cannot be
preserved without a
general knowledge
among the people.

—John Adams

Conformity is
the jailer of
freedom and the
enemy of growth.

-John F. Kennedy

The flag is the embodiment, not of sentiment, but of history.

341

-Woodrow Wilson

I have never had a feeling politically that did not spring from the sentiments embodied in the Declaration of Independence.

—Abraham Lincoln

A democracy is more than a form of government; it is primarily a mode of associated living, of conjoint communicated experience.

—John Dewey

This will remain the land of the free only so long as it is the home of the brave.

—Elmer Davis

Our flag has never waved over
any community but in blessing.

—William McKinley

Let freedom
never perish in
your hands, but
piously transmit it to
your children.

-Joseph Addison

America is rising with a giant's strength. Its bones are yet but cartilages.

-Fisher Adams

347

You can't separate peace from freedom because no one can be at peace unless he has freedom.

—Malcolm X

Freedom has a thousand charms
to show, that slaves, howe'er
contented, never know.

—William Cowper

Democracy…is a condition where people believe that other people are as good as they are.

—Stuart Chase

The world must be made
safe for democracy.

—Woodrow Wilson

A house divided
against itself
cannot stand.

-Abraham Lincoln

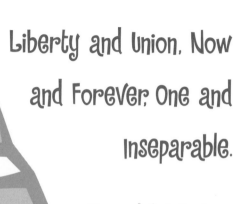

Liberty and Union, Now and Forever, One and Inseparable.

-Daniel Webster

353

You can't prove you're an American by waving Old Glory.

—Helen Gahagan Douglas

Peace is a blessing, and like most blessings, it must be earned.

—Dwight D. Eisenhower

You make men love their government and their country by giving them the kind of government and the kind of country that inspire respect and love.

—Zechariah Chafee Jr.

357

Liberty does not consist, my fellow citizens, in mere declarations of the rights of man. It consists in the translation of those declarations into definite actions.

—Woodrow Wilson

Your country needs you!

-World War I
recruiting slogan

Freedom lies in being
bold.

-Robert Frost

After all—it's a
great country, but
you can't live in it

for nothing.

-Will Rogers

The best energies of my life have been spent in endeavoring to establish and perpetuate the blessings of free government.

—Andrew Johnson

361

Our "pathway" is straight to the ballot box, with no variableness nor shadow of turning…We demand in the Reconstruction suffrage for all the citizens of the Republic. I would not talk of Negroes or women, but of citizens.

—Elizabeth Cady Stanton

There is one thing better than good government, and that is government in which all the people have a part.

-William Hines Page

America, the land
of unlimited
possibilities. 364

-Ludwig Max
Goldberger

We the People of the United States, in Order to form a more perfect Union, establish Justice, insure domestic Tranquility, provide for the common defense, promote the general Welfare, and secure the Blessings of Liberty to ourselves and our Posterity, do ordain and establish this Constitution for the United States of America.

—The Preamble to the U.S. Constitution (1787)